Peace
BE
STILL

Peace
BE
STILL

ROSHARNA
STEWART

PEACE BE STILL

Scripture quotations taken from the Amplified® Bible (AMP),
Copyright © 2015 by The Lockman Foundation
Used by permission. www.Lockman.org"

Scripture taken from The Message. Copyright © 1993, 1994, 1995, 1996, 2000, 2001, 2002. Used by permission of NavPress Publishing Group

THE HOLY BIBLE, NEW INTERNATIONAL VERSION®, NIV® Copyright © 1973, 1978, 1984, 2011 by Biblica, Inc.® Used by permission. All rights reserved worldwide.

Scripture quotations marked (NLT) are taken from the Holy Bible, New Living Translation, copyright © 1996, 2004, 2007, 2013, 2015 by Tyndale House Foundation. Used by permission of Tyndale House Publishers, Inc., Carol Stream, Illinois 60188. All rights reserved.

Tree of Life (TLV) Translation of the Bible. Copyright © 2015 by The Messianic Jewish Family Bible Society.

Front Cover Photo: Tate Photographic Imaging
Back Cover Photo: Yolanda Rouse Photography

iUniverse books may be ordered through booksellers or by contacting:

iUniverse
1663 Liberty Drive
Bloomington, IN 47403
www.iuniverse.com
1-800-Authors (1-800-288-4677)

ISBN: 978-1-5320-4208-9 (sc)
ISBN: 978-1-5320-4209-6 (e)

Library of Congress Control Number: 2018901567

Print information available on the last page.

iUniverse rev. date: 06/01/2018

I dedicate this book to my parents, my deceased loved ones that meant the world to me, my former students, anyone that's apprehensive of stepping out on faith, and to music!

Contents

As a single woman going through various phases of life (joy, pain, growing, change, love, betrayal, distrust, forgiveness, loving myself, and even more), I have learned so much about the power of prayer! I received some visions and promises from God that have required me to believe in God and stand strong in my faith. One main event in particular brought me to my knees and thus developed my strong relationship with God. As a result, I began to write about the different occurrences of my life related or unrelated to the promise. I remember thinking about what should I do? How do you handle this type of situation? Many times I couldn't go to my parents, friends, or family. I was driven to get on my knees and pray. This book is for every woman or man who may have doubts, fears, worries, or concerns in life. It is my prayer that God gets the glory through every entry! Please understand that this is about my life and my experiences. The sole purpose of this devotional is to show everyone that trusting and having faith in God is key and that no matter the situation or circumstance, God can give you peace and a word in the midst of it ALL!

In closing, I encourage you with this scripture as it has helped me to endure the process of writing this book and share my story. **But he said to me, "My grace is sufficient for you, for my power is made perfect in weakness." Therefore, I will boast all the more gladly about my weaknesses, so that Christ's power may rest on me.** 2 Corinthians 12:9 10 (NIV)

Instructions:

This devotional is interactive (hands-on)! It will require you to look up the scripture, and answer questions accordingly. Once you're done, you will write on your sticky-note to create your "War Room". I personally used this method after watching the movie "War Room". If you have not seen the movie, I highly encourage you to! I hope to inspire you to begin to write and proclaim what thus says the Lord! I'm certain that during and after this devotional time, His word and Promises will be made evident in your life!

You will need: a bible (or app), a pen/pencil, and a sticky note pad or an index card to post for your "war room" when you're done.

1. Scripture Focus

2. Scripture (Writing) Activity

3. Life Application (How it applies to you)

4. Prayer (War Room) Entry: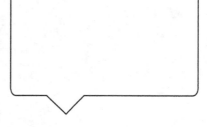

Have you ever been in a season of life where you're trying as much as possible to trust God but all sorts of things come up in your life and you're forced to prove if you really can trust Him and truly be at peace? Well that's where I am and for those of you who don't understand, let me explain. I've been writing this book (that I felt God told me to write) for several years. I've started, stopped, and had many breaks in between. My season of storms started when I became sick with a simple stomach virus. We all know what the entails, however the pain never left almost three weeks later and I began to physically see a knot on the right side of my stomach. I kept going to the doctor paying several co-pays in an effort to figure out what's going on. Meanwhile I had people who were past due from repaying me a large sum of money. This resulted in affecting my household and my livelihood. Thankfully my bills were paid for the month but I could no longer pay to go to the doctor or simply put gas in my car and I was forced to ask my parents for help. At thirty-something years old this wasn't the best feeling. During this time of sickness, I was weak and could not sleep. The enemy attacked my mind and made me think I had a disease and that I was going to die. I would cry, pray, and ask God for his help. I've gotten lab test, consults, CT scans and all trying to figure this all out on top of juggling work, church, responsibilities, and just people in general. It was in this moment that I realized this needed to be the first entry of this devotional. All of this happened so that I could share my story with you and to encourage you to understand that the storms may rage but you can be at peace because you have the Lord in your "boat" with you! Peace be still!

Scripture Focus: Matthew 8:23-27 (MSG) *Highlight key words:* *Then he got in the boat, his disciples with him. The next thing they knew, they were in a severe storm. Waves were crashing into the boat—and he was sound asleep! They roused him, pleading, "Master, save us! We're going down!" Jesus reprimanded them. "Why are you such cowards, such faint-hearts?" Then he stood up and told the wind to be silent, the sea to quiet down: "Silence!" The sea became smooth as glass. The men rubbed their eyes, astonished. "What's going on here? Wind and sea come to heel at his command!*

Write down the topics or issues that are keeping you from having peace.

_____

_____

_____

Write this prayer: God I thank you for giving me peace over _____.
Lord your word tells us to stand on your promises. So I turn this/
these issue(s) over to you! Just as the scripture states, Lord help me
to be at peace and to rest even when there may be turmoil around
me. Most importantly may you get the glory out of this and show
yourself mighty through this situation. I claim it settled and done in
Jesus Name I pray, Amen.

God is so good! I can remember hearing a Word from Him and I struggled with obeying God because I couldn't figure out what the end result was going to be. God has even instructed me to cut people out of my life that I didn't want to let go. I learned after several attempts that "obedience is better than sacrifice". When I made up my mind to trust God and thought about the consequences of disobedience, not even 24 hours later God moved. He knew in my heart that I had a made up mind to obey what He said. I encourage you that when God says to move or let go, do it. I know it may be hard but understand that He knows the plans that He has for you. THERE'S GREATER IN FRONT OF YOU! Peace be still!

Scripture Focus: 1 Samuel 15:22-23 (MSG)

Write the scripture and underline words that speak to you!

_____

_____

_____

_____

What is something in your life that you need to get rid of or even perhaps press pause on?

_____

When your **heart is ready and you can be truly honest with God**, write a prayer asking for forgiveness and tell Him how you're ready to obey!

I remember when someone dear to me did something that hurt me. I really get irritated when I'm there for someone but when I need help or support that same person is unavailable for me. Sometimes when you don't release this type of stressor, it can bring on resentment. Dealing with pasts hurts can be tough. It could be a "letdown", family arguments, or even church hurt. There is a scripture that talks about letting God be your refuge. God sees, knows, and I believe that He can even feel our hurts and deepest pains. His word encourages us to still have hope and know that He will fight our battles, even when it doesn't feel or look like He is. So let this encourage you and began to meditate on the word that he promised us and see how God Will Move!

Scripture Focus: Psalms 46:1 (NIV)

What does the scripture state? Underline key words from the scripture.

_____

_____

_____

What is hurting you today?

_____

_____

_____

Whatever is hurting you today, write a prayer <u>thanking</u> God that He is your <u>refuge</u>.

What if God told you to go? What would you do? Would you really go or would you think of all the many details of how, where, when, and why? I can remember when I was in my early twenties God told me to quit my job and pursue teaching. I was already in school pursuing my master's in education but I was working in a job that had nothing to do with the education field. But when I heard God so clearly I was so confident that I stepped out on faith and quit my job. I stopped working in May, by the end of July I signed a contract to become a teacher. I remember someone dear to me strongly disagreeing with my decision to quit. I tried explaining to this person that The Lord told me to and I wasn't received very well. Later I prayed and asked God to show himself mighty into my situation.

God has told many of you to "Go". It may be to go back to school, to move to a new place, to marry the one you love, to preach the Word of God, or to even take a new job. Believe in Him that he will direct your path. In the bible, God instructed Abraham to go away from his country and go to a new land that He will show him and God promised to bless him. The text doesn't say whether Abraham pondered on the instructions it just said that he obeyed. God wants a yes from you when He tells you to go. Trust that God knows and holds your future. Yes, going to the unknown can seem scary. However, when you realize who you serve, He'll make the steps easier once you make the first step. In time it will make sense so "Go" and be on purpose for The Lord! I recommend while you meditate and pray to listen to the song "I Give Myself Away" by William McDowell. It's a great worship song that is perfectly aligned with today's devotional.

Scripture Focus: Genesis 12:1,4 (NIV)

Verse 1 - The LORD had said to Abram, "_____
_____."Verse 4 - So Abram went,_____
_____; and Lot went with him. Abram was seventy-five years old when he set out from Harran.

GO – I need to "Give Obedience" in this area: _____

As you write your prayer, reflect on the goodness of God. When you ask does he not supply? Be willing to "**G**ive **O**bedience" today in your prayer!

It's 4:45 a.m. and I've been up for about 45 min. I'm under attack. I can't sleep. I've had insomnia for about a week. A friend of mine dropped some news to me about a week ago and ever since then I haven't been able to sleep. The enemy's attack kept my mind replaying the situation over and over. I'm constantly crying and trying to get peace because I also have to go to work and attend rehearsals in the evening as well. Have you ever worried or had a situation to consume you so much that you can't eat or sleep? Or when you do sleep, the slightest thing wakes you up and all of the worries and cares of life dump right back on you the minute you wake up. As I'm currently trying to encourage myself at almost 5 o'clock in the morning, I encourage you to pray, take a hold of God's word, His promises, and know that this is temporary! The word says to meditate on His word day and night! So if you're under spiritual attack know that you're more than a conqueror! God will get glory out of this and His word promises that you are already victorious! I recommend listening to Israel Houghton. He is an awesome praise and worship minister who has produced hundreds of songs. Listen to any of his songs when you're feeling attacked or struggling and need peace! Peace be still!

Scripture Focus: Romans 8:26 (NIV)

Write the scripture:

_____

_____

_____

At this particular time, I was stressing, worrying, and upset about things that I couldn't control. The enemy would attack my mind so much that I couldn't do anything sometimes but just moan and pray. Have you been there before? Write down some suggested solutions on what you can do when you're being attacked.

Solutions:

1.	2.	3.
4.	5.	6.

> Write down a prayer claiming your victory when the enemy tries to come into your mind and tell you what you're not! Write your prayer claiming who and what you are!!!

It's funny to me how the enemy will try to make you see things in the natural. But it's amazing how Gods eye is totally different from that. We have to ask God to give us a glimpse of what He sees to help increase our faith. Now this will happen when you spend time with him and truly have relationship with the Lord. There's a story in the bible that talks about dry bones. Ezekiel the prophet tells how the Lord took him to a valley and with the natural eye there appeared to be dead people, a valley of bones. But God saw something different. God told Ezekiel to first speak to the dry bones and command for them to have flesh and muscles and then he commanded breath over them. Just as he commanded the bones came to life. These bones are a representation of everything that seems dead in your life that God has said he would give to you. The Lord doesn't want you to keep looking at it with your eye but with His eyes and command it to be! So profess the word of God and fill in the blank of whatever it is that looks dead, and remember God is bringing it back to you all He wants you to do is speak life over it!

Scripture Focus: Ezekiel 37:1-14, key verse 12 (NIV)

What does the scripture say?

_____

_____

_____

How can you use God's eyes to help you in your situation?

_____

_____

_____

Just as the scripture states, what is dry in your life/ looks dead that God has the power to resurrect? Is it lining up with the word of God? Let your prayer be aligned with his word and learn to focus on the power of God!

I remember a few years ago that I wanted a change of environment badly. I was tired, frustrated, and overwhelmed. Well this move didn't go through and I was highly upset. Since I was still in my current environment, the entire year I didn't put my all into what I was doing. Because I was so determined about changing my environment, I dwelled on what was not happening and had an attitude about it. As time went on and I stayed in my current situation I noticed how things began to turn around. It wasn't perfect but it was better. I prayed and studied and I changed my attitude to a servant's perspective and realized that this is where I'm supposed to be and I'm going to remain optimistic. Well I found out later that the environment that I wanted so badly was actually worse than where I was. I praise God for that because He knows and holds our future. God says He will not withhold any good thing from you so trust Him when an opportunity doesn't go through for you. He could be protecting you because it may be worse over there than where you currently are.

Scripture Focus: Psalms 84:11 (NIV)

*Psalms 84:11 says "For the L*ORD *God is a _____ and _____; the L*ORD *bestows _____and _____; no _____ thing does he_____from those whose walk is_____."*

Identify areas in your life that you need to change your perspective. (I've started your list with prayer!

1. <u>Prayer</u> 2. _____ 3. _____ 4. _____

1. Prayer

Using this shape, write down your list of what you're going to change in triangle. Give yourself some ideas or suggestions of ways to stick with changing your perspective. I've listed one for you.

It's the New Year! I'm so excited for a fresh start and I'm so optimistic to what this new year has to offer. I promised myself that I wouldn't bring last year's issues into the new year, but somehow someway they seem to creep back in. I'm praying that all strongholds, burdens, and worries leave and that I be set free in Jesus name! It's funny when you're a kid you plan that your life will go a certain way. But oh when reality sinks in and you see where your life is you realize that one, two, (or maybe more ☺) of those things, actually happened as planned. Seek and pray and ask God what is His will for your life. As a year ends I always try to reflect on the year and how I can improve. I also ask God what is His desire for me? I write the things that I hear God say. Next I pray and thank Him that He's bringing it to pass! Align your life to what He wants instead your own. Watch and see…when God writes the story of your life, the narration is greater!

Scripture Focus: Matthew 6:33 (AMP)

Write down today's scripture:

_____

_____

_____

Have you created your life situations? Is your life where you want it to be? Based on this devotional and scripture today, what have you learned that you need to do?

_____

_____

_____

Write a prayer to God surrendering your will over to His will!

We all have dealt with people that in some shape or another have hurt us. I encourage you to maintain your Christianity and be that light that shines for Him. I've had people to truly hurt me to the core because they hurt those closest to me. How do you handle being around people that hurt you or those important to you? Stay in faith and watch how and where God is moving. He will provide an opportunity to show you how He will and can move.

There may come some times in life where words and actions of others will hurt you, but The Lord wants to remind you to not be of the world but act according to what he has commanded you to be.... "a light that sits on the hill!" You want to always be like salt and **keep your flavor**. God is using you so don't lose sight of your purpose!

Scripture Focus: Matthew 5:14-16 (NIV)

Fill in the scripture: ¹⁴ *"You are the_____ of the world. A town built on a hill cannot be _____. ¹⁵ Neither do people light a lamp and put it under a _____. Instead they put it on its stand, and it gives _____to _____in the _____. ¹⁶ In the same way, let your _____ _____ before _____, that they may see your _____ _____and _____ your Father in _____.*

In what areas or environments do you need to start letting your "light shine" so that others may see your good deeds?

_____

_____

Copy this prayer for your War Room:

Lord as I come to you today, I need your help in the area of _____. I desire to let my light shine despite what others may say or do. Help me to rise higher and not succumb to the ways of this world. Instead help me to think of ways to sow good deeds so that you get all of the glory, honor, and praise.

Do you consider what you do a ministry? You should. How many times have we all said, "I don't want/feel like going to work....or I'm not in the mood to do much today.....The people that I'm around are getting on my nerves! I can't stand my _____ ." We can all relate that at some point in our lives we have at least said one of these statements. Despite our wants, maybe it's our purpose to be on the current job that we hold. There may be someone that works with us that doesn't know Jesus. As an educator, I realize how impactful I can be. By sowing seeds of love for example, God mandated us to love. It's one of the greatest things that we can do. I see how important it is that children get a good example of what love should be. I've also learned that sometimes building permanent relationships with others, specifically some of the kids, was for me as well! Many times we forget and get caught up in our own wants that we neglect to ask God if we are on assignment for Him to get the glory. We ultimately were created to serve. Don't forget that someone is watching you. Don't lose your testimony and message because you haven't changed your attitude from "what I want" to "Lord, thy will be done." God will reward you for your obedience!

Scripture Focus: Colossians 3:24-25 (MSG)

Highlight or underline words that stand out in the scripture: *"Servants, do what you're told by your earthly masters. And don't just do the minimum that will get you by. Do your best. Work from the heart for your real Master, for God, confident that you'll get paid in full when you come into your inheritance. Keep in mind always that the ultimate Master you're serving is Christ. The sullen servant who does shoddy work will be held responsible. Being a follower of Jesus doesn't cover up bad work."*

What's your ministry? What comes easy to you? Is it time to refocus your lens at work into a ministry mindset instead of just doing a job?

_____

_____

_____

> Write a prayer asking God for help with doing your best at work. Thank Him for the opportunity to share the Love of Christ everywhere that you go!

Have you ever had unspoken issues with people? Whenever you're around each other you feel the elephant in the room? Well I have struggled understanding why some people are in each other's face, pretending and knowing that they like someone when they don't. The individuals who taunt others to purposely get under another person's skin. I have wondered for so long why do people bring each other down so much but I've learned that it's usually about their own personal issues that I can't control. I have found it imperative to pray often and ask God to keep me in perfect peace because sometimes my flesh wants to react in an ungodly manner. How many people can relate to trying to be level headed, staying wise, and most importantly let your let shine but you keep getting tested over and over? I encourage you to stay grounded in the Word of God, to pray constantly, and not let the devil have you succumb and react in a "worldly" way. God sees what's going on. Trust and know that He will protect you! He will work those situations out so that you won't have to take matters into your own hands! Peace be still!!

Scripture Focus: 2 Chronicles 20:17 (NIV)

Write the scripture:

_____

_____

_____

Sometimes God has you in situations to develop your character! We cannot control other people's ways, thoughts, and etc., but we can control ours. What is God trying to develop in you right now?

_____

_____

_____

Write your prayer thanking God for developing you! Remember, God wants the best you so that He can be glorified!

Have you ever awakened in the middle of night and couldn't go back to sleep? Did you know that it's usually God waking you up? He's trying to get your attention. He wants you to spend time with Him. This is the time to pray and read the Word (Bible) and hear what thus says The Lord! In the still of the night or early morning, he awakens you. It's usually the time when everyone is asleep and no one can distract you. I encourage you to spend time with God and hear what He has to say. It will bless you and possibly someone else too. Just like with any earthly relationship, in order for you to be close, you have to spend time with them and you go through things together. The same thing happens with your relationship with God. You go through ups and downs. There have been sudden blessings that you didn't see coming, ways that He has made provisions for you that you just couldn't see how it would work out. There will be times when you don't have anyone but Him. And that's what He wants, to remind you who is always there. To show you through both good and bad I'm always with you! As you reflect in church, at home or etc., it will be easy to wave your hand, shout hallelujah, and to cry out unto him. As you strengthen your relationship with God, he will begin to use you more and more. Develop that relationship.... it's the best relationship that you will ever have!

Scripture Focus: Isaiah 50:4 (NIV)

The Sovereign _____ has given me a well-instructed _____, to know the word that _____ the weary. He _____ me _____ by morning, wakens my ear to _____ like one being _____.

Write these things down as reminders when you're awakened while you're sleep.

1. What does God want me to know?

   _____

2. Have I prayed and asked God for guidance/direction?

   _____

3. Is my bible near me so that I can read?

   _____

> If you're awakened in the middle of the night, it may be God trying to get your attention. He wants a relationship with you! In your prayer, thank Him for these moments, you'll never know what He's trying to share with you! It may feel like an inconvenience, but know that it's love!

Unfortunately, I have experienced some tragic things in my life. Honestly, I still have hang ups with these situations. I don't constantly think about them, but every year around the time that these situations happened, I notice my "PTSD" kicks in and I begin to struggle. I'm tired of being "stuck" in situations that happened years ago. Sometimes I have learned that things happen to make you stronger, wiser, and to help others! I didn't want to put this in the book but I know I have to. It's my job to learn from them, get back up, and help others along the way as I walk this journey of life. What are you hurting from that has taken a while to get over? It didn't happen on accident. God knew you could handle it because you are still here standing, living, and impacting others! Don't let the issue(s) keep you from living!

Scripture Focus: Psalms 55:22 (NIV)

The scriptures says, _____

_____

What are you still hurting from that you need to release to God?

_____

_____

> How can you use your situation to help others and give God the glory? Write your prayer on these things and watch God move! The pain will slowly go away all because you gave it to God!

Has God ever given you a picture of your life and you can see it so vividly? Well that's similar to me. I can see portions of my life and I get excited that God shares these things with me. One of those visions that I have received is seeing myself married. Right now I'm going through a period where I feel alone, and lonely. I've been praying to God for a long time for my husband. I've asked God what I need to do....is it something I'm not doing...I don't know. What I do know is that I'm a hopeless romantic. I desire to truly be loved, adored, and to have a faithful man. I believe God knows my heart and has placed those very desires inside of me. Even though I feel alone, I know that God is with me. I have to trust the plans that He has for my life even when I don't understand. So as I encourage myself, I encourage others who are waiting and desiring things from God to remember that waiting develops strength. Though the vision may tarry....wait for it! It's going to happen...but in God's time, not our time!

Scripture Focus: Habakkuk 2:3 (TLB)

And the _____ said to me, "Write my _____ on a billboard, _____ and clear, so that _____ can _____ it at a glance and rush to tell the _____. But these things I _____ won't happen _____ _____. Slowly, _____, surely, the time approaches when the _____ will be _____. If it seems slow, do not _____, for these things will _____ come to_____. Just be _____! They will not be _____a single _____!

As you reflect over your life what is it that you see through your spiritual eye that God has shared with you? Believe God for it and write it down!

_____

_____

In your prayer closet write your prayer to God for the vision God has shared with you that has yet to come to pass!

Have you ever had one of those days where anything and anyone can just set you off? Today was a rough day for me at work, anything and everything that could irritate me did. Now when I got up, I had a great morning at home. I prayed and got ready for work feeling good, but the minute I came into the door at work the irritants were lined up one after the other to begin a horrible day for me. I struggled all day trying to readjust my attitude. (By the way, I'm fasting. Which means I'm hungry also!) I'm sure my testimony was gone! I'm writing today to encourage us to stay firm in the word and not let the tricks of the enemy sway us. We all have our days, however, don't give the enemy grounds to steal your joy! My friends, be of good courage and of good cheer, and dismiss that negative energy!

Scripture Focus: 1 Peter 5:8 (AMP)

Be _____ [well balanced and self-disciplined], be _____ and cautious at _____ times. That enemy of yours, the devil, prowls around like a roaring lion [fiercely _____], seeking someone to _____.

What things in life have you possibly fallen to due to the tricks of the enemy? Write them down.

_____

_____

_____

What in your life are you ready to reclaim and take back from the schemes of the enemy? Write your war cry/prayer thanking God for equipping you to handle any situation that may come! Remember you are VICTORIOUS!

Getting rid of an addiction or cutting off an addiction is very hard. In life there are so many things that we can get "comfortable" with and it becomes an addiction. We are used to it, it is a part of us, and at it times, we even crave for it. Some of us may be dealing with addictions such as shopping, drugs, food cravings, people, social media, or even things like video games. God wants to know ultimately that you will give it up to be close to Him. At my church, we are doing a fast, the Daniel fast. (Which means eating no meats, only fruits and vegetables.) I am really realizing how much meats are a part of my daily diet. Sometimes I truly crave the desire to eat some meat. I often want to break down and cheat and get a little meat. That's what our flesh does, those comfortable things that we just love so much and so used to having can be an addiction. It's powerful if we can show or tell God...."Lord you know I love _____, however I'm willing to give it up just to get closer and to hear from you. "Can you deny yourself, take up the cross, and follow The Lord?"

Scripture Focus: 1 John 2:15-17 (MSG)

Complete the scripture: Don't _____ the world's _____. Don't love the world's _____. Love of the world _____ out _____for the _____. Practically _____that goes on in the _____ —wanting your own _____, wanting everything for _____, wanting to appear _____ —has nothing to do with the _____. It just _____ you from _____. The world and all its _____, wanting, wanting is on the way _____ —but _____does what _____ wants is set for _____.

Lord I'm willing to give up _____-_____ for more of you!!!

Before you write you prayer there's an old hymn called "I Surrender All". If you can find it listen to the song and read the lyrics. Give God your everything and pour out to Him in your prayer.

I can't sleep! So many things were on my mind so I thought that I would write. I have to confess that I have anxieties in certain areas, due to experiencing various things. If only people could see how their actions create distrust and distrust has the potential to affect the offended person in various ways. Although I try to press on, it's hard to forget the hurt, pain, lies, and for me there's a fear that it's going to happen again. It seems difficult for people to recognize, own, and understand their own faults. I know that this is yet another situation that I have to keep on living and hope that God moves. Have you experienced some sleepless nights? Tossing and turning over things that you can't control? Wishing that people can feel and understand the pain that they've caused? Well this was where I was, I was struggling with wanting them to see and know how their actions have hurt me, and it wasn't being grasped. How do you convey hurt to family, friends, and etc.? I encourage you to release it to God!!

Scripture Focus: Luke 6:27-36 (key verse 28) 2 Chronicles 7:14 (NIV)

Write the scripture Luke 6:28: _____

_____

It's definitely hard when someone doesn't understand or gets the pain that they've caused. I know it seems so simple but the word of God tells us to simply pray for those individuals. Your freedom over this situation can happen instantly when you pray. God can begin moving as soon as you give it to Him. I can assure you this…as soon as you start consistently praying for the person/people, in His time you will see change and you will be released from the issue! Who do you need to pray for and what is it that you need to release to God? _____

_____

_____

Write your prayer to God for the person or people who have hurt you. Ask God to help those individuals to understand the hurt that they've caused and in the end you'll end up thanking God for your "growing pains".

Do you know how important it is to fellowship with one another in the body of Christ? We need each other to encourage and build up, to pray for one another, and to simply be there for each other. As one body in Christ, we also have had our share of struggles and strains! It is so important that we share our stories with both the saved and unsaved! I know it can be scary to let your story "out". There are thoughts that come into your mind about who to trust and who can you share your story with. For some of us, sharing our innermost issues can be unsettling especially with people you know (and can be judgmental) as well as those individuals you don't know. However, we have to trust God. Many people don't realize how our struggles and stories are truly to help someone else. My brothers and sisters, don't be afraid to share your story, God will show you who to tell and when to tell it. He will also tell you who you should not talk to. We are all fighting on the same side, so if we can help loose someone else and set them free; then ultimately God gets the glory. This is the ultimate goal. So let's help build one another in the body of Christ and learn to be transparent amongst those to whom we are assigned to.

Scripture Focus: Psalms 66:16 (NIV)

Write out the scripture here:

_____

_____

What are your testimonies that you're withholding? Is there something that you can share with others to show God's goodness, mercy, or love? Write them down.

_____

_____

_____

As you reflect on God's goodness in your life, make a commitment to be a witness and share what God can do and has done in your life with others!

I am one of those people who like to be transparent with those I consider myself close to. Can you relate? I do this to often show them my weaknesses, my flaws, and to show simply that I'm human. I struggled for a while because I spoke with someone that I could confide in at a particular time and some of the things that this person said I totally disagreed with. It was almost border line offensive. How do you handle people that you've shared intimate, personal stories and it seems as if they're judgmental? My flesh wanted to go off but because of who this person was, I couldn't do that. Regardless of what others feel or think I have to be reassured and stand on the fact that if God said it, then He said it. That settles it. Peace be still!!!!

Scripture Focus: Romans 14:1 (MSG)

_____ with open _____ fellow believers who don't _____ things the way you do. And don't _____ all over them every time they _____ or _____ something you don't _____ with—even when it seems that they are _____ on _____ but weak in the _____ department. Remember, they have their own _____ to deal with. _____ them _____.

Have you ever condemned someone or have felt/been condemned by someone? Write down what happened and tell how you got through it.

_____

_____

_____

_____

Write a prayer to God telling Him you won't let others make you doubt. Stay strong and courageous because God will see you through! You will be victorious!

Prophetic Poem Written by: Ms. Rosharna Stewart

Stop wondering always if I'm here,
For I want you to know that I'm always near.
I've seen, I've heard your despairing cry....
In the middle of the night asking me why Lord, why?
Well here's your answer after all this time,
I had to get you back, you forgot that you were mine.
Live on purpose and do as I say,
And I promise you this, your spouse will come God's way.
Yes, it is a poem but God can speak through them too,
Have faith and believe because I said I will see it through.

My son/daughter remember that you are a king/queen,
All this time I was getting them cleaned.
Pure and whole and just for you,
To be a witness for me and a partner for you.
Many great things together you'll do,
The world you will see and your kids will too.
The key is to know that you are a chosen one,
My anointed son/daughter, whose new life has just begun.
Remember to live on purpose and pass the test,
And Every Dream and Every Desire will be an amen and a yes!

Write the scripture: _____

_____

_____

_____

This poem is very special to me. God gave me this at a low point in my life. I believe every word. This poem came from wounds, crying, anger, and hurt. God will restore and rebuild you! I can personally attest to His amazing love! This poem wasn't only meant for me but for you as well! This is not limited to a spouse! It's whatever you believe God has promised you! Remember to believe because God has already said "YES" and "Amen"! Peace be still!

> What stood out to you in this poem? Thank God for your promise and believe it shall come to pass. Write a prayer to God thanking Him as if you have already received your promise!

In my own devotional and prayer time, I read the book of Ruth. It's a short book with so many profound messages. I believe that this story can be inspirational not just for women but men as well. In my reading, I discovered that Ruth was noticed while she was working. Ladies and gentlemen, I encourage you to be on purpose for The Lord. Walking in your assignment is where you're supposed to be. When you're where you're supposed to be (walking in obedience) that's when you will notice how things fall into place. Ruth wasn't worrying about anything else, she was working to make sure she had food for herself and Naomi. Second, it says in the fourth chapter, that someone else, by right, was supposed to get the land and also assume the responsibility of Naomi and Ruth. But that individual didn't want Ruth in addition to the land and Naomi. God can move those who may seem like they're "in line" for the position, house, promotion, man/woman, or etc. But trust that what God has for you is for you! The Lord worked it, He knew the plan for you even when it seemed impossible. Be encouraged your "inheritance" is on the way! Peace be still!

Scripture focus: Ruth 4:6 (MSG)

Write the scripture. _____

_____

_____

What inheritance are you believing God for? _____

_____

> Write your prayer to God thanking and asking Him for your "inheritance". If you're not sure about what your "inheritance" is, ask him to reveal it to you! I'm certain that He will!

Being in love is a wonderful feeling! Meeting someone who impacts your life the most and being able to share your life with them is priceless. Nothing feels better than loving the person that God has sent you. In relationships, we have to be careful of the promises that we make to others because there are many times when we don't fulfill our end of the promise. Sometimes promises/commitments requires people to make big leaps and sacrifices. It took me experiencing being hurt by people to appreciate and understand the hurt I may have imposed on others. Man or woman I encourage you, if you're not fully committed or making unfulfilled promises, then don't waste people's time and don't use them. It's definitely not of God! Treat people the way you want to be treated! If you've wronged someone take a step back, look at their feelings and how things have impacted them. Find it in your heart to reconcile and watch God heal the hurt and bring you even closer to God than you were before.

Scripture Focus: Psalms 34:18 (NIV)

Write down the scripture: _____

_____

Have you mistreated a loved one, taken advantage of someone, or didn't value a person that now you regret mistreating? Write it down and then write what you can do to fix it. Problem(s):
_____

Solution(s): _____

Write down a prayer to God apologizing for hurting his child! Using the scripture, write in your prayer ways that you can change in the future.

Have you ever seen people who gossip excessively, who are deceitful/fake, or just generally messy? Can you feel the lack of genuineness every time they approach? I have as well. I struggle with why people hate on one another, talk about each other, and enjoy "throwing shade". We should be lifting one another up, praying for each other, and being genuinely supportive. I shared this because it's real and it's a trick of the enemy to divide God's children and to keep us from being true vessels for Him. Not that I am perfect or have never done any of the qualities above; I do try my hardest not to portray these characteristics.

On the other hand, how do you deal with people when you can hear them talking about you or pretending to like you? It's difficult to react in a Christian-like manner when people act this way towards you. However, if we respond in the flesh, we know that God will not get the glory out of it. Today's devotional is for the real people who can attest and understand how many issues in life can take you to a place that you know you don't need to be. But because of your love for Christ and the seriousness of your walk, you know the best way to handle these situations are to pray for them. Peace be still my sister/my brother!

Scripture Focus: 1 Peter 5:8-10 (NIV)

Highlight key phrases in the scripture: *"Be alert and of sober mind. Your enemy the devil prowls around like a roaring lion looking for someone to devour. Resist him, standing firm in the faith, because you know that the family of believers throughout the world is undergoing the same kind of sufferings. And the God of all grace, who called you to his eternal glory in Christ, after you have suffered a little while, will himself restore you and make you strong, firm and steadfast."*

Don't allow others to make you lose your witness! Write down ways that you can rise above falling for the enemy's tactics and schemes.

_____

_____

Write a prayer to God telling him how you plan to rise above pettiness, immaturity, and jealousy. Tell God how you plan to be an example of what He represents!

The spirit of The Lord is upon me in a heavy way. I constantly get chills and I've been in a true worship space. My body is going through changes.... I have a knot under my arm, abdominal pain but yet I praise Him. The doctors were concerned and wondered if it was a lump. I chose to believe that it wasn't. God gave me a message twice in one day. I read it in a daily devotional and the second time I heard that same scripture in a message from Joel Osteen. The message stated being a miracle for someone else. Now mind you, I have my own situation going on, and the message is telling me to help someone else? Have you ever noticed that while you're going through, God will use you to be a blessing to someone else? Don't walk by when you see an opportunity for God to use you even while you're dealing with your own issues. Stop and be a vessel to help meet the need for someone else.

Scripture Focus: Proverbs 11:25 (NIV)

Write what the scripture states: _____

_____

Make a list of some people you can be a blessing to. Pray and ask God what you can to be a miracle in their life.

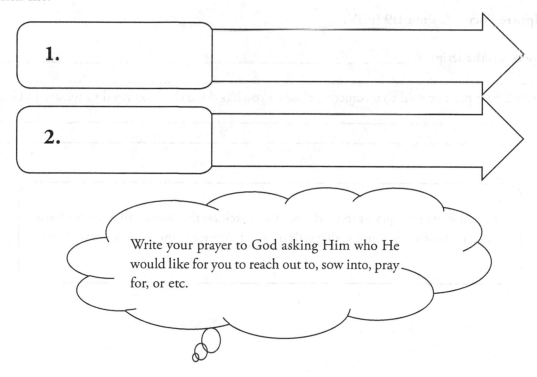

1.

2.

Write your prayer to God asking Him who He would like for you to reach out to, sow into, pray for, or etc.

As I lay in my bed and think of so many things in my heart, one just seems to permeate in my spirit. In recent years I've developed the unhealthy habit of worrying and harboring on things that I can't control. As I continue to grow, I've been asking God to give me peace over things that I can't control. Someone that I love is doing something that truly hurts, I've tried communicating it, but I know when a person has a made up mind to do something, they're going to do it. However, ever since I was small I've never wanted to disappoint people and there have been a lot of things in my life that I've wanted to do but stopped myself because I didn't want my actions to hurt others. I'm at a point in my life where I'm upset for making choices to spare others when my feelings aren't being considered or factored. Now I know that in time God will allow this to be an opportunity for us to mend, heal, and talk. But in this journey I believe that God shows us that even the closest ones to us will hurt us to some extent. God truly has to show us who is sovereign, never changing, and ultimately the one to depend on. The scripture says that He will never leave you or forsake you. Be encouraged today that yes even our parents, siblings, spouse, friends, or the closest people in our lives may let us down, but there is a God who will always be there and never leave your side. He'll be a father to the fatherless and a mother to the motherless. No matter the situation God can fit the mold and/or fill the void!

Scripture Focus: Joshua 1:9 (NIV)

Write down the scripture._____
_____

Is there a past pain or void that someone close to you has done that you need to release to God?
_____
_____

As you write your prayer to God, ask Him to release the issues, hurts, or concerns that you have with someone that is dear to you. Always know that God is with you.

As I sit in my bed, I think and reflect in a spirit of loneliness. There are often times in my life when I look around at everyone else and notice how they have a significant other. Most of my friends are either married or in serious relationships. I remember one weekend I went to Atlanta with two of my closest friends. I was taking a shower and when I came out, everyone was on the phone with their significant other. It felt like a ton of bricks hit me because I truly felt the feeling of loneliness. The thought, "you don't have anyone" began to permeate in my mind. For the first time, instead of feeling sorry for myself, I prayed to God. I asked Him to remove the emotion/feeling. I told God that I trusted Him and I know that my husband is on the way. I thanked Him and I immediately began to feel better! Single woman/man of God, His word will not come back void! Though the vision may tarry wait for it! God has your spouse, and they're on the way! Be encouraged and Peace be still!

Scripture Focus: Romans 15:4 (NIV)

The scripture says: For _____ *that was written in the* _____ *was written to* _____ *us, so that through the* _____ *taught in the* _____ *and the* _____ *they provide we might have* _____*."*

I need encouragement in the following areas:

Write a prayer to God thanking Him for the encouragement in the areas that you listed above. (Just wait! You will start receiving them! He's going to blow your mind!!)

How do you get out of something that you feel trapped in? You don't want to hurt anyone but you know what's best for you. The Lord will give us specific instructions but we are fearful of hurting people, worrying about what they may think, and we don't simply have the strength to know how to just do it. Have you worried about other people and their feelings? That's been an issue of mine, but I'm praying that God would free me from worrying about what others think. Have you ever worried or put too much emphasis on others when your focus needs to be on God? God's instruction takes higher precedence than anything else. You may not see a way out through your lens, but trust that God knows how the ending will be.

Scripture Focus: Galatians 1:10 (NIV)

What does the scripture state? Underline key words.

_____

_____

_____

Do you worry about what other people think? Are you letting others keep you from obeying God? How can you change your mindset and change your actions?

_____

_____

What I Want:	What God Wants:	What I need to do now:
	Obedience	
	_____	
	Excellence	
	Love one another	
	_____	

Write down the scripture in your prayer and make your allegiance to God claiming that you will do what pleases Him and not man!

Although I have never physically birthed a child, I do tend to love children as if I did. I can remember concerning myself over a situation with someone very special to me. Parents how do you handle seeing your baby grow up? How do you handle tough situations that they may find themselves in and there's nothing you can do but pray? With one situation in particular, I had to release this child to God. It's definitely not easy to do, but in order for me to be at peace, I realized that I had no other choice.

Parents, aunts, uncles, siblings, godparents, and etc., are you having a hard time letting go of your children or those dearest to you? Is it hard to let them live their life? Do you want to protect them from as much as you can? These were questions that I had to answer. Trust God with him or her. Regardless of your role, remember that you planted the seeds and trust that God will provide the harvest! Moses' mother gave him up as a baby to give him a chance at life, and I'm sure it was hard! However, his mother released him and it ended up working out for his good! Peace be still!

Scripture Focus: Exodus 2:1-3 (MSG)

A man from the family of _____ married a Levite woman. The woman became _____ and had a _____. She saw there was something _____ about him and _____ him. She hid him for _____ months. When she couldn't hide him any longer she got a little _____ made of papyrus, _____ it with tar and pitch, and placed the child in it. Then she set it _____ in the reeds at the edge of the _____.

Are you willing to trust God with your child or a child that is very dear and special to you? Write down some ways that you can start showing God that you trust him concerning this area of life.

_____

> Write a prayer to God telling him that you will learn how to trust him even with your child/children or those that are dear to you! Tell him that you release him or her to him! It's hard I know, but remember no one will love and protect them like God!

Wow life has been pretty busy I have not made time for my writing. Since my last time here I've had three deaths in my family in a matter of six weeks, a beloved church member died and it really shook up the church, and I took in someone dear to me for about 6 weeks. In addition to all of this, I've even been stressed at work. The praise report through it all is God has kept me! I praise Him for this. I'm learning more and more what the seasoned saints mean by "Jesus kept me". I don't know how I was juggling it all and still was able to function but I'm so grateful that He loves me and gave me the grace to handle this season!!

Mark 11:22-25 Talks about embracing God and being able to boldly and confidently say to a mountain to be moved and it will go....whatever you're facing or going through in life it's so important to be in relationship with God. His word promises to keep you and encourages us to believe and pray and we have the power within us to move those blockages simply because we are connected to God! Peace be still even in the midst of trying times!

Scripture Focus: Mark 11:22-23 (NIV)

Have _____ in God," Jesus answered. "Truly I tell you, if _____ says to this _____, 'Go, throw yourself into the _____,' and does not _____ in their _____ but _____ that what they _____ will _____, it will be _____ for them.

What are your mountains today that you are facing?

_____

_____

_____

At times life can throw us some curve balls! But God has given us victory to speak over those "mountains". Some of those "mountains" we have no control over, but we still can remain resilient in Him. Write your prayer to God thanking him for the victory that has already been won!

Today was a great day!!! I finally had the opportunity to meet with someone today!!! All week I had been going to God about what to say. I was nervous but God helped make it so easy to talk to this person. It was very liberating because the person said that what I was saying is just confirmation for them. There is nothing like being used for the Lord. I can remember prior to this day coming how I was rethinking over and over what to say how to say it, and etc. I had to learn how to be led by the Holy Spirit and let Him speak through me. I truly want to be used by God to help his people, and I pray for more opportunities to be used by Him. What have you been apprehensive about with God when He gives you an assignment? Be bold, confident, and strong in the Lord for kingdom building! Hearing God can be challenging at times especially when you hear God telling you to say something to someone. You don't want to be wrong, you don't know if they are going to receive it, and you don't want to look crazy. However, this is what this journey is all about! Are you willing to look crazy for God? There are so many stories in the bible where God used people in some impossible situations. The Lord told people to say and do things that definitely sounded crazy or weird, but he showed himself mighty in every situation. Don't let the tricks of the enemy and doubt seep into your mind. Be prayerful and harken unto his voice, the Lord will tell you exactly what to do or say!

Scripture Focus: Exodus 9:1 (NIV)

Then the LORD said to Moses, "Go to _____ and say to him, 'This is what the LORD, the God of the Hebrews, says:
"_____."

What do you sense God telling you to say to someone? You could possibly be a blessing to someone just by sharing what he told you to say! In your prayer time write what you hear God saying.

_____

_____

_____

In your prayer time write your War Room entry telling God you want to hear him more and you want to be used by Him. Watch God will begin to speak to you and through you!!!

It's 2:41 a.m. I haven't been sleeping good for a while. I toss and turn. My mind runs constantly on different things and I feel like I'm alone, with no one to truly understand and being constantly attacked. Lord, my strength wavers from one end to the next. Where are you? Deliver me from this insomnia! My heart is broken and I need to be repaired. Only you can heal me, but I can't feel you near me. Your word says that I'm never alone....for you are always with me....but where are you?

Help me! I will never forget this place...I will help others who have been hurt, rejected, broken, or etc. If you've been here before don't give up on Him! He will come in and rescue you...the attack is only temporary. God knew that you could handle it...He knew that you would seek Him. You will come out victorious. Your tears matter...your hurt matters...your pain is felt by Him. His grace is sufficient for you!

(If I'm honest I'm nervous about sharing my inner most thoughts because I feared how I would be perceived. But God told me that it's ok to show my weaknesses and to share my weaknesses because by me sharing and opening up to you I show how strong my God is!)

Scripture Focus: 2 Corinthians 12:9 (NIV)

But he said to me, "My _____ is _____ for you, for my _____ is made perfect in _____." Therefore, I will _____ all the more gladly about my_____, so that Christ's _____ may rest on _____.

Our imperfections are opportunities to show how strong and mighty our God is. Let God's power rest on you! What are your weaknesses or hang ups in life? Are you willing to own them and change? Can you see how it is all connected to giving glory to God?

_____

_____

_____

Weaknesses can hold us back and distract us from where God wants us to be. Write a prayer to God about your distractions, and ask for help and sustaining strength through Him!

Personally, singing songs is an antidote for me to feel better through many situations. I find myself listening to the lyrics, the movement of the notes, moving to each beat of the music, and I find that it takes me to a place that I just can't seem to put into words. Through the good and the bad I often listen to Christian or gospel music to sing praises to God or to just help me when I'm faced in a tough or uncomfortable time. It is often stated in the bible that God wants us to sing to him, to honor him, and give praise and worship to him no matter the situation. What if nothing's wrong? You're in a season where things are going well. Do you still remember to praise God? Men, is this an easy task for you? Can you praise or worship God when you've recently been bombarded with an unexpected expense/situation? Women, how often do you go to God to sing to Him when you're happy, upset, angry, or content with life? If we're all honest, we usually don't respond to God first, we react to the situation! I encourage you and myself to remember to praise God for the little things, i.e. waking up, having food to eat, etc., and to remember, let praise and worship be your response when unexpected things occur!

Scripture Focus: Ephesians 5:19 (AMP)

_____ to one another in _____ and _____ and spiritual_____, [offering _____ by] _____and making _____ with your _____ to the _____;

Man/Woman learn how to sing praises unto him despite the situation. A great album to listen to is Trey McLaughlin and the Sounds of Zamar. On the album is a great song entitled *"I Will Praise"*. The song talks about praising God when you're feeling alone, confused, and even when things are ok. Write down some opportunities that you can give God your best through song below:

_____

_____

> Write a prayer to God simply thanking Him with your current state on today, whether it's a good day or bad day! Next, I encourage you to listen to the song/album above. I'm sure it will bless you!

One year around December, God gave me a word that was very intimate and personal. I'm not going to release it; however, it spoke of change and a very specific scripture and topic. I was released in April to talk to the intended person about it and it opened so many doors. I personally was scared to release this because I wanted to be sure I was saying what God said. Keep in mind the conversation was given in April, now let's fast forward three weeks which is now a Sunday. My pastor, Rev. Dr. Charles E. Goodman, Jr. spoke from the exact scripture that I gave to the person and the topic. I was so excited because this was my confirmation about how God speaks to me. And I was excited because I knew God was speaking. He ordained this and I cried with tears of JOY!!! Because He loves me so much he sent this word as a confirmation for me and it was an "on time WORD!!!" Be encouraged and be at peace because he will give you what you need and He's TRULY an on time God! His promises will come to pass!

Scripture Focus: Hebrews 6:15; 17-18 (NIV)

Write verse 15 – _____

_____

Verses 17-18 - *Because _____ wanted to make the _____ nature of his _____ very clear to the _____ of what was _____, he _____ it with an _____. God did this so that, by two _____ things in which it is _____ for God to _____, we who have fled to take hold of the _____ set before us may be greatly _____.*

In this scripture, God confirmed what he told to Abraham and He will do the same for you if you stand and wait patiently in faith. What is it that you're waiting on God to do in your life? What has He promised that hasn't happened yet?

_____

_____

_____

Waiting sometimes isn't fun, but are you willing to stand in faith while God is working on your behalf? Write your prayer to God thanking Him for moving and confirming the promise that He placed in your heart.

Forgiveness is a word that's huge to me. It's something that God wants us to do to our fellow brothers and sisters. It's also something that He does for us on a daily basis. When I think of all the mistakes and mess ups that I've done in my life I begin to cry out because I know I shouldn't even be alive. God is such a mighty God and His grace and mercy keeps us even when we shouldn't be kept. Think back over your life on some of the things that you've done or said that may have hurt God, others, or even yourself. Even in our disobedience God still loves us and forgives us of our sins. What if God didn't forgive us just as some of us haven't forgiven the hurt or pain that other people have put on us? God wants that same measure of forgiveness for others that He gives to us when we ask for forgiveness. Who is it that you haven't forgiven for a past hurt? Go back and reconcile with that co-worker, parent, sibling, spouse, or friend. God says in order to be forgiven you must first forgive. When you do it, watch and see how more doors will open up in your life. Remember, we block blessings for ourselves when we harbor in unforgiveness.

Scripture Focus: Mark 11:25 (AMP)

Write the scripture: Whenever you stand_____, if you have anything against_____, forgive him [_____the issue, let it_____, so that your_____ who is in heaven will also_____ you your_____ and wrongdoings [against_____ and_____].

This is such an important topic. Is there someone in your life that you need to forgive? I challenge you to write a letter to the person/people (if you decide to give it to them, it is totally up to you) and take this time to pour your heart out and openly and honestly forgive them! Don't let what someone else did or didn't do keep you from missing out on your blessings!

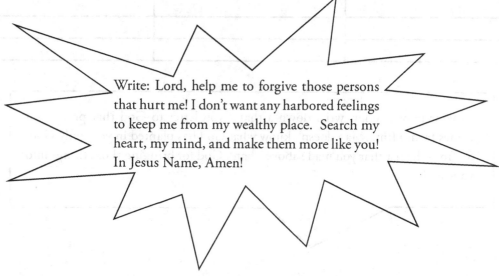

Write: Lord, help me to forgive those persons that hurt me! I don't want any harbored feelings to keep me from my wealthy place. Search my heart, my mind, and make them more like you! In Jesus Name, Amen!

One year I received an email and phone call stating that I got a new position. Now this was truly a time of change for me. I was very nervous about this new move because it involves unfamiliar territory....i.e. new people, new job, duties, and new culture. In life, you'll find that God will put you in unfamiliar territory. It's crazy because my first day meeting everyone I heard various comments. I heard things like "we don't need all of these new people...I heard they just let anybody get the job." Now my flesh wanted to share some words with them but I have to know when to rise above negativity and this was certainly a time. I knew it was nobody but the enemy. These types of schemes were tactics to make me feel inferior, and to make me doubt this promotion that God has given me. I was already having thoughts of nervousness and feeling overwhelmed about the position but I know that God is with me and will guide me along the way. What has God given you that others may feel you don't deserve? Remember the word says promotion comes from God not man! Peace be still!

Scripture Focus: Psalms 75:6-7 (NIV)

*Write down the scripture:*_____

_____

_____

Is there something in your life that you're believing God for that others don't think you deserve or should pursue? Write down your list of things that you believe God has given you or has already given you.

In your prayer today, write down a thank you letter to God that promotion comes from Him. Man doesn't know what God has planted in you, only God. So from the list that you made above, thank God for bringing those things into your life!

What do you do when the death of a loved one comes unexpectedly? What if it's a child that hadn't had a chance for life? It's hard to accept the phrase, "God makes no mistakes", when it's people that are close to you. The Lord said He wants you to know that He sees the pain, but everything that happens is ultimately for His glory. He says our thoughts are not His thoughts and our ways are not His ways. Throughout life we forget that we were actually created for Him so that He gets the glory in all that we do. Be confident that your loved one served his/her purpose and that their death can possibly even be a wakeup call for others to get their lives aligned with Christ. Let's not forget we are called to a greater calling and standard which is Jesus Christ our Lord and Savior. Although you're hurt and in pain God will ease the sorrow in time and your strength will be renewed in Him! Praise Him even through this and see God move even during times of pain!

Scripture Focus: Isaiah 43:7 (MSG)

What does this scripture say? I _____ them back, every last _____ who bears my name, every man, _____, and _____ Whom I _____ for my_____, yes, personally _____ and made each one.

Has there been a tragedy or a significant loss in your life that you need God's help with? Write it down. _____

_____

_____

Pour your heart out to God by completing the sentence. Write your prayer expressing your need for help and that you understand that we ultimately were made for His glory!

God I need your help concerning the loss of _____.

As a Christian we have to remember that our walks are going to be attacked daily because we are on purpose for The Lord. My number one struggle is staying firm in the word and believing what God said. It's amazing how God and I will have an awesome experience together and He gives me a word/promise to stand on. The next day at work, home, or even church, the enemy will attack my mind and allow me to "see" how what God promised me won't happen. There have also been times when I try to control the situation to make it happen.

God loves it when we rest in Him. He can't get the glory in anything that we try to make happen. He is an omnipotent, omniscient God and it pleases Him when we show God that we trust Him, we have Faith in Him, and we believe that He will do just what He said. God has given you some promises such as healing, a child, a spouse, a job, house, or etc. Your promise may even be something intangible such as peace, joy, or love! God says stop trying to figure out how it can happen and let me show you just Who I Am! I am going to blow your mind! There's a scripture that talks about being planted by a river even in intense, heated times like a tree. God is our source (water) and we need to be like that tree that's planted by that river so that even in the hottest (hardest) times we stay confident and at peace because we know who supplies all of our needs. God will give us what we need and give us the promises that He said He would give us. It's going to happen! Stay rooted and rest in Him!

Scripture Focus: Jeremiah 17:7-8 (NLT)

But _____ are those who _____ in the _____ and have made the Lord their _____ and _____. They are like _____ planted along a _____, with roots that _____ _____ into the _____. Such trees are not _____ by the _____ or _____ by _____ months of _____. Their _____ stay _____, and they _____ stop _____ fruit.

What are the "heated situations" that is keeping you from believing? You must know that God wants us to trust Him and believe that He will do it. Write down the things that "appear" to be hindrances in your life.

_____

_____

> As you create another entry of your war room, let this prayer be a commanding prayer claiming the things that you listed above will not waiver your faith anymore!

It's almost 5 am today, I was awakened from a dream I had so I decided to write. Yesterday I was out with either food poisoning or a 24-hour stomach bug. It's amazing to me because the day before yesterday I was so focused and driven about getting this book together I was able to create the first 10 pages. I felt so focused, determined, and somewhat accomplished. I was blocked yesterday with this stomach issue but I praise God that I'm still here and able to proceed with my heart's desire to get this book done. Ladies and gentleman don't let anything block you from what God instructed you to do. Yes, there may be a few road blocks along the way (such as my temporary illness), but be so driven that you know God's going to allow you to finish the "good work" that He placed inside of you! What is it that God has placed on your heart for you to do? Are you willing to push through despite the road blocks? Don't let these temporary occurrences stop you! Seek His peace and keep going!

Scripture Focus: Philippians 1:6 (AMP)

I am _____ and _____ of this very thing, that _____ who has begun a _____ _____ in _____ will [_____ to] _____ and _____ it until the _____ of Christ _____ [the time of His _____].

What is in your heart that you feel God wants you to do that you haven't yet started on or finished?

1. _____
2. _____
3. _____

What are you going to do next to make sure you complete your good works?

_____

_____

When you're serious and ready! Write your prayer to God about the things in your heart that you feel He wants you to start. He will lead and guide you to the people, things, and places that you will need! I'm confident and believing in you! You can and will finish!

As I sit and think of how God has brought me so far, I'm amazed and at awe. My strength is unparalleled, and the forgiveness in my heart is pure. My God has brought me a long way! I finally feel like my life is lining up in the direction that God sees fit. My prayer life and bible study is back to where it used to be. My desires and prayers have been "Lord, let your will be as it may." However, if I'm honest, there are a few things that I do desire greatly. I'm trusting and believing in God and that He will do it, without delay! I encourage you that as you partake on this journey of life, the most important thing that you can do is be a participant in your relationship with God! He will lead, guide, direct, and protect you on the way that you should go or not go. You will have an inner peace and a feeling of wholeness even if some of the things you want you haven't received yet! God is the answer to everything. Get Him first and everything else will fall into place. Search for the Lord and You Will find HIM! Peace be still!

Scripture Focus: Jeremiah 29:13 (MSG)

Highlight or underline key words in the scripture: *"When you come looking for me, you'll find me. "Yes, when you get serious about finding me and want it more than anything else, I'll make sure you won't be disappointed." GOD's Decree. "I'll turn things around for you. I'll bring you back from all the countries into which I drove you"—GOD's Decree—"bring you home to the place from which I sent you off into exile. You can count on it.*

There is a song by Israel Houghton and New Breed called "I Will Search". As you meditate on today's devotional, listen to this song and let it minister to your spirit! After listening ask yourself are you truly seeking after God? What can you do as a result of today's devotional?

_____

_____

> Write your prayer telling the Lord that you are seeking after Him! Be encouraged because you will find Him if you truly give Him your heart!

Prophetic Poem Written by: Ms. Rosharna Stewart

I proclaim that my new life starts today!
I am expecting to get my _____ (fill it in) God's way.
I'm standing on the promises of God,
I know He will do it; He's my staff and my rod.

He's restoring everything that was taken from me,
For the enemy has tried to make me feel defeated intentionally.
For I know that this word will come to pass,
He's promised it over and over to ensure that my faith would last.

I'm ready to sing all praises to you,
To proclaim to others that you'll see them through!
My brother/sister stay strong in your word,
Don't allow what you have seen to keep you deterred.

Our Father He knows that you would believe,
That's why it's in you, He placed the dream.
He knows that He can trust you so fight with faith,
Even when others don't see it, and are quick to debate.

It's Here! It's Here! Can you see it now?
Can you hear His Voice? He's (God has) made His vows.
Your promise has come and been made evident,
You and the world will see that the Lord has fulfilled His covenant!!!!

As we end the 40-day devotional, I proclaim God's promises over your life! It is my prayer that you've been able to reflect on God's goodness and how to remain in faith and have peace, despite the circumstances of life! This poem was birthed actually while I was going through various things in life. I was carrying a load of emotions feeling crazy with a lot of self-doubt, and uncertainty but deep inside I still felt that God spoke to me. Just when I was ready to give up or turn away that's when I felt very full and I began to write. God spoke through me to tell me **it's coming and the time is now!** I didn't go through this just for myself, it was for you too, and therefore I share this poem with you! Your victory is coming, your healing is coming, your promises are coming, and it's all coming now! I pray that you were blessed, uplifted, and greatly impacted through this book!

*Joshua 21:43-45 Key scriptures (AMP)

Additional Scriptures: Numbers 23:19 and Ezekiel 34:25-31 (AMP)

Scripture: So the _____ gave Israel all the _____ which He had _____ to give to their fathers (_____), and they took _____ of it and _____ in it. The LORD gave them _____ [from _____] on every side, in accordance with _____ that He had _____to their _____, and not _____ of all their _____ stood before them [in _____]; the LORD _____ _____ all their enemies to them. Not _____ of the good _____ which the _____ had _____ to the house of Israel _____; _____ had _____ to _____.

What stood out in the poem? What words in the scripture meant something to you? Ask God to reveal what He wants you to receive from this poem.

_____

_____

_____

_____

Declared Promise

It is finished! You've created a 40-Day Prayer and Promises War Room and your faith is being renewed! As you read the poem, write your prayer (or better yet, declare your prayer) as if it's already done!

Remember, PEACE BE STILL!!

Printed in the United States
By Bookmasters